AF552355

Unmasking Mormonism

DAVE HUNT &
ED DECKER

HARVEST HOUSE PUBLISHERS
Eugene, Oregon 97402

All Scripture quotations in this book are taken from the King James Version of the Bible.

UNMASKING MORMONISM

Taken from **THE GOD MAKERS**
Copyright © 1984 by Dave Hunt and Ed Decker
Published by Harvest House Publishers
Eugene, Oregon 97402

ISBN 0-89081-801-0

All rights reserved. No portion of this book may be reproduced in any form without the written permission of the Publisher.

Printed in the United States of America.

1

Could Such Good People Be Wrong?

Jim and Judy were typical converts to the Mormon Church. Although they had been active in a mainline Protestant denomination for years, they had never found that deep personal relationship with God that they sensed they needed and longed for.

In the course of his business, Jim came into contact with an active and zealous member of the Church of Jesus Christ of Latter-Day Saints. Feeling themselves drawn to this man and his beautiful family, Jim and Judy gradually became more and more involved with them socially. There were so many good qualities evident in the relationships in this Mormon home that Jim and Judy began to wonder whether these people might not have found the answer to that hunger for God that still gnawed deep within their own hearts.

"These people seemed to be Christians," Judy told us. "Any people that I'd ever been around that I had felt were really Christians had the same attributes. They were fine, good, loving, family-oriented people."

Not only were the relationships of family members extremely close and loving, but they noticed something else: They took their religion very seriously. This made Jim and Judy think that perhaps these people really did have what they had been seeking.

Jim picked up the story at this point. "At our friends' request, the missionaries came to see us and we began to take the lessons. As they would leave each night, they would encourage us to read the Book of Mormon and to pray that we might know whether it was true. At the end of the six lessons, we were encouraged to be baptized into the Mormon Church. However, these two precious young men told us that they weren't going to ask for a definite answer that last night. Instead, they would wait until the following night to see what we had decided. In the meanwhile, most of the Mormons in Mesa, Arizona, would fast and pray that our answer would be the right one."

"They were so sincere about this," added Judy. Her voice reflected both an appreciation and a sadness. "The next day Jim and I each received so many calls! Mormons we'd never met phoned me at the apartment and Jim at work. The voice on the line would say, 'This is brother and sister so-and-so. We're fasting and praying for you that your answer will be the right one.' We were sure impressed that they were a very loving people. When the missionaries came back to ask us if we wanted to be baptized, we couldn't help but say *yes*!"

It was only after several years that Jim and Judy began studying the Bible and asking God's guidance and at last realized what they were *really* involved in. The experience almost cost them their marriage. The true facts about Mormonism were entirely different from what they had been led to believe. Joining had been easy, reinforced as it had been with so much love. Getting out was something else. What they had thought was genuine love expressed over and over by Mormons who had become their closest friends suddenly turned to a severing of relationships and false accusations.

More Than Family

The Mormon Church has worked very diligently and successfully not only to project worldwide a wholesome family image, but to present itself as the only true representative of Christianity upon earth. Though most people reject that claim as extravagant, they are left with the impression that Mormonism is simply an extreme form of Christian fundamentalism. Nothing could be further from the truth. On the contrary, Mormonism is a modified form of paganism which is so carefully camouflaged with a facade of Christian terminology that it even deceives most Mormons. Paganism is the universal naturalistic religion of the human race. It usually involves communication with spirits, a hierarchy of many gods, and appeasement of these powerful beings through occult rituals leading to the mastery of forces inherent in nature.

Paganism, Mormonism, and the Fall of Man

Strangely enough, rather than being ashamed of the obvious fact that Mormonism is paganism revived, leading Mormons have pointed this out themselves. Mormon authority Milton R. Hunter has written:

> Mormon Prophets have continuously taught the sublime truth that God the Eternal Father was once a mortal man. . . . He became God—an exalted being—through obedience to the same eternal Gospel truths that we are given opportunity today to obey.
>
> The Mystery Religions, pagan rivals of Christianity, taught emphatically the doctrine that "men may become Gods."
>
> Hermes declared: "We must not shrink from saying that a man on earth is a mortal god, and that God in heaven is an immortal man."
>
> This thought very closely resembles the teachings of the Prophet Joseph Smith and of President Lorenzo Snow.[1]

So Mormonism openly aligns itself with what its own leaders identify as "pagan rivals of Christianity."

The central belief both in Mormonism and paganism is the ancient dream that men can become gods. Jesus called Satan "a liar and the father of it"—i.e., the father of *the* lie. No greater lie could be conceived than that humans could become Gods. Eve was deceived by the Serpent's seductive offer of godhood. Adam wasn't deceived, but he nevertheless joined the rebellion instigated by Eve's seducer because he didn't want to lose his wife.[2] The Bible makes it clear that this sin of disobedience destroyed both Adam's and Eve's relationship to God, thereby bringing instant spiritual death and eventual physical death upon them and all of their descendants.[3] None of us can complain, however, because we have each rebelled against God in our own way, and we deserve the penalty: "The wages of sin is death."[4]

In contrast to the consistent teaching of the Judeo-Christian Scriptures, pagan/occult traditions consider the seduction of Eve to be a blessing in disguise. This allegedly made it possible for Adam and Eve to have children and unlocked the door to godhood for them and their descendants. Sterling W. Sill, Assistant to the Council of the Twelve Apostles, expressed Mormonism's agreement with pagan/occult mythology when he wrote:

> Adam fell, but he fell in the right direction . . . toward the goal . . . he fell upward.[5]

In Latter-Day Saints (LDS) doctrine the ancient lie that destroyed the human race has metamorphosed into the central truth. It is loudly trumpeted by the Mormon General Authorities again and again. President Joseph Fielding Smith stated it in these words:

> The fall of man came as a blessing in disguise . . . I never speak of the part Eve took in this fall as a sin, nor do I accuse Adam of a sin. . . .
>
> We can hardly look upon anything resulting in such benefits as being a sin. . . .[7]

Having accepted the fall of man as necessary and beneficial, both Mormonism and paganism honor the lie that seduced Eve and avidly pursue the "Godhood" which the Serpent promised. The central purpose in occultism is to achieve mastery of various psychospiritual techniques that lead to "realization" of the godhood that the Serpent promised. Mormonism has its own formula involving secret rituals that must be performed repeatedly in the Mormon Temple, but it is basically derived from ancient pagan traditions.

Gods-in-Embryo, Spirits-in-Waiting

Mormonism declares that we are all uncreated "gods-in-embryo" who have been progressing eternally upward in various forms and stages of ever-higher development in the spirit realm. Though literal sons and daughters of a "Mother and Father God,"[8] for some inexplicable reason we aren't "Gods" by birth, but were required to come to this earth to take on a physical human body in order to prove ourselves worthy of godhood. Infinite numbers of our spirit ancestors have successfully earned their full godhood in this same manner and now rule as gods and goddesses over untold trillions of worlds like ours.[9]

Although the farthest reaches of the universe are now allegedly peopled with gods and goddesses with physical, resurrected bodies that were once mortal, Mormonism teaches that there are still multitudes of full-grown adult spirits out there waiting for bodies to inhabit so that they too can become gods.[10] President Joseph Fielding Smith taught that there is "possibly no greater sin" than any form of birth control.[11] This is why it is the duty of every righteous Mormon husband and wife to produce as many babies as possible. Only then can these waiting spirits come to earth to earn their full and rightful deity.

Although unable to remember anything of a fabled "preexistence" in the spirit world, every true Mormon must nevertheless believe in it because he has sworn to uphold Mormonism's founding Prophet, Joseph Smith. It was Smith who claimed he had received revelations about this premortal state from god-men who allegedly put us here and live on a distant planet near a giant star called Kolob. According to young Joseph, one of his extraterrestrial visitors, a god-man with a physical body (sometimes called "Elohim"), claimed to be the very Father of the spirits of all humans, and claimed that we had lived with him on his home planet before being sent to earth.

Why is nothing of the preexistence remembered? Early Mormon Apostle Orson Pratt explained:

> When all these spirits were sent forth from the eternal worlds, they were, no doubt, not infants; but when they entered the infant tabernacle [body], they were under the necessity, the same as our Lord and Savior, of being compressed, or diminished in size so that their spirits could be enclosed in infant tabernacles. . . .
>
> . . . When he [man] enters a body of flesh, his spirit is so compressed and contracted in infancy that he forgets his former existence. . . .[12]

The LDS church teaches that it was in the preexistent world that Jesus and Lucifer, two elder "brothers"[13] (sexually begotten sons of God as we all are),[14] vied before the "council of gods" for the honor of becoming the Savior of mankind. The plan that Jesus proposed was approved by the council's majority vote. In anger, Lucifer drew one-third of the brothers and sisters into rebellion against the council's decision. He then became the Devil and his followers the demons.[15]

Mormons believe this amazing tale because of their "testimony" that Joseph Smith was a true prophet inspired by visiting god-men. Those who have some doubts would not be very likely to admit it, for that would cost them their passport to heaven. Most Mormons rest happily in the confidence that the amazing eternal future that Joseph Smith promised is no less certain than the fabled eternal past he described.

2

Sifting Fact from Fancy

Any attempt to form a rational understanding of the actual history of Mormonism involves the dizzying unraveling of contradictory accounts of fantastic events in a mind-numbing, frustrating journey through what Walter Martin has called *The Maze of Mormonism*.[1] This effort to sift fact from fancy is made all the more difficult by the countless changes in "revelations" and personal accounts, effected by the Mormon hierarchy without notice. The saga of the "First Vision" is a prime example.

The official account now published by the Church alleges that in 1820, when he was 14 years old, Joseph Smith "saw two Personages whose brightness and glory defy all description, standing above me in the air. One of them spake unto me, calling me by name, and said—pointing to the other—*This is my beloved Son. Hear Him!*"[2] Seizing this unusual opportunity to ask which church he should join, young Joseph was told that he "must join none of them, for they were all wrong, and . . . all their creeds were an abomination in His sight. . . ."[3] This "vision" is crucial to all of Mormonism's claims. It is in the first lesson the Mormon missionaries teach to prospective converts, and a "testimony" of its authenticity is a prerequisite for baptism. The following foundational Mormon doctrines are implicit in this vision: 1) that God is a man with a physical body; 2) that the Father and Son are two separate Gods each with His own body; 3) that there had been a total apostasy, leaving all churches in hopeless heresy; and 4) that Father and Son had put in their first and only appearance on earth together in the history of mankind for the specific purpose of calling this young boy to "restore" the truth by founding the true Church.

There are a number of glaring contradictions in this story. The official account that the Church relies upon today was not published until 1842, some 22 years after it was alleged to have occurred. Surely no Mormons should complain if this fact causes a great deal of skepticism. Assistant Mormon Church historian James B. Allen admits that during the 1830's "The general membership of the Church knew little, if anything, about it [the First Vision]."[4] Dr. Allen states that:

> . . . none of the available contemporary writings about Joseph Smith in the 1830s, none of the publications of the Church in that decade, and no contemporary journal or correspondence yet discovered mentions the story of the first vision. . . .[5]

In view of the above, any prudent person would be compelled to strongly suspect that the alleged "First Vision" is pure fiction concocted many years after it was supposed to have happened. Many other facts point in this same direction.

If Joseph Smith had seen God the Father in a physical body as a glorified man in 1820, why would he have approved the "Lectures on Faith" that declared the Father to be "a personage of Spirit?"[6] The "Lectures" were incorporated into Mormon scripture in 1835 and remained there until 1921, when they were quietly removed without explanation. And if Smith had seen Father and Son in two separate bodies in 1820, why would the "Prophet" in the mid-1830's (in the course of rewriting the entire Bible to correct alleged errors in translation) change Luke 10:22 to read (as it still does in the Mormon "Inspired Version"), "that the Son is the Father, and the Father is the Son"?

The statement by the "Personages" in this vision that all of the Christian creeds on earth "were an abomination" also doesn't ring true. The Apostles' and Nicene Creeds that were accepted by most Christian churches in 1820 simply state such basics as belief "in God the Father Almighty, Maker of Heaven and earth . . . in Jesus Christ, His only Son, our Lord, who was conceived by the Holy Ghost, born of the Virgin Mary, suffered under Pontius Pilate, was crucified, dead, and buried, and resurrected" etc. One wonders what could be an "abomination" in creeds that are so Biblical and even in agreement with what Joseph Smith himself believed for at least another ten years after this alleged vision. Stranger still is the fact that Joseph Smith and his family at that time were heavily involved in necromancy and divination, communicating with spirits of the dead and divining the location of buried treasure, which the Bible in no uncertain terms declares to be an abomination to God. What "God" could this be who has no word of reproof for Joseph's necromancy and divination, yet abominates all Biblical creeds? Could this be why the "truth" that "God" calls Joseph Smith to "restore" turns out to be identical to the *lie* that Satan used to deceive Eve?

Joseph the Methodist

One of the strangest contradictions in the entire episode of the alleged First Vision is the fact that, having been twice forbidden in this same vision by the Father to join a church, the young "Prophet," who by this time has had many angelic visits, has been led by the angel Moroni to discover a number of gold plates covered with hieroglyphics and is translating the Book of Mormon from these plates, proceeds in 1828 to join the Methodist Church in Harmony, Pennsylvania. Joseph's wife, Emma, had been a Methodist since the age of seven, so Joseph may have joined the Methodists to please her—but join he did. There are only two possibilities: 1) Joseph Smith was an incredibly disobedient and irresponsible "Prophet" and his "God" extremely forgetful in not reproving him for joining the Methodist "abomination," or 2) the First Vision didn't really happen, but was invented later.

The Hidden Account

In the confused and contradictory roots of Mormonism, there are nine different accounts of the "First Vision," each of which contradicts the others on major points. As Sandra Tanner, a former Mormon who is one of the foremost living authorities on Mormon history, remarked when we interviewed her for the film *The God Makers*:

> He [Joseph Smith] changes the date, he changes how old he is, he changes the motivation, why he went into the woods to pray. He changes who was there and he changes what the message was that they gave him.
>
> If he were giving us an actual account of a real experience, we would assume he would have known the first time around whether it was God or Jesus, if it was both of them, what their message was, and when it happened.

The one thing that all the nine accounts (except the revised 1842 version) agree upon is that Joseph Smith in none of them claims to have seen God the Father, much less in a physical body. Yet this is the major point now made by the Mormon Church in what has to be a classic case of deception. For 130 years they kept hidden the one and only account written in Joseph Smith's own hand. Copies finally leaked out, and it proves the blatant and deliberate deceit behind this whole scam. Apparently written about 1833, in this account Joseph tells of a *heavenly vision* of the Lord (Jesus), *not an earthly visit* of Father and Son; and it is the Lord in heaven who says, "Joseph my son, thy sins are forgiven thee," *not* the Father who says, pointing to Jesus, "this is my beloved Son."

A hymn that Joseph Smith approved, loved, and sang—"An angel from on high the Long, Long Silence broke"—refers to the "First Vision." Still sung today, its very presence in the Mormon hymnal is an indictment of the dishonesty of a Church that builds its claim to world domination on a lie so gross that the contradictions are still there to haunt believers after decades of suppression, revision, and deception.[8]

Joseph the Glass-Looker

Long before Joseph Smith allegedly was led by the angel to the ancient gold plates, he had already established a wide reputation as a "seer" who, in the words of his mother, Lucy, "possessed certain means by which he could discern things invisible to the naked eye."[9] Joseph's mother relates that because of this remarkable talent, a certain "Josiah Stoal [sic] came from Chenango County, New York, with the view of getting Joseph to assist him in digging for a silver mine."[10] The Mormon historian B.H. Roberts says of Stowell: "Having heard of Joseph Smith's gift of seership, he came to the Smith residence to employ him . . . Joseph [Smith] hired out to Mr. Stoal [sic] . . . and for something like a month they vainly sought to find the 'hidden treasure' . . . Joseph continued for some time in his employment."[11] A local citizen of the area at that time, W.D. Purple, relates:

> In February 1826, the sons of Mr. Stowell, who lived with their father, were greatly incensed against Smith, as they plainly saw their father squandering his property in the fruitless search for hidden treasures . . . and caused the arrest of Smith. . . .[12]

W.D. Purple was present at the trial, and his careful notes of the entire proceedings were later published in *The Chenango Union* of May 3, 1877. Mormon apologists rejected W.D. Purple's account as spurious and tried to deny that their founding Prophet, at the same time the angel Moroni was allegedly appearing to him annually in preparation for leading him to the buried golden plates, was hiring himself out to locate buried treasure by means of a "seer stone" that he used like a fortune-teller's crystal ball. After spending 20 pages trying to discredit the idea that Joseph Smith had ever been arrested for "glass-looking," Dr. Hugh Nibley, dean of Mormon apologists, conceded:

> . . . if this court record is authentic, it is the most damning evidence in existence against Joseph Smith . . . the most devastating blow to Smith ever delivered. . . .[13]

The devastating blow fell July 28, 1971, when Wesley P. Walters and Fred Poffarl together discovered in a mildewed box in the darkest part of a basement storage room beneath Chenango County jail the records of Judge Albert Neely and Constable Philip M. DeZeng.[14] These proved once and for all that Joseph Smith had indeed been arrested and found guilty on March 20, 1826, of pretending to find buried treasure by "glass-looking."

The "Seer Stone"

Young Joseph Smith had found his "seer stone" while on a dig. It was brown and about the size of an egg, and is still held by the Mormon Church, safely locked away.[16] There is no record that Joseph Smith ever actually recovered any buried treasure, but many reports that he and the other "glass-lookers" located all manner of valuable finds that kept "sinking deeper" in the earth as the diggers pursued them. There was always an "explanation" about some enchantment or spirit that prevented the treasure from being taken, and there were always enough superstitious people who believed this sort of nonsense to keep Joseph Smith and numerous other "glass-lookers" in business during the early 1800's.

Upstate New York was filled with people who were ready to believe almost any tale, the taller the better. Buried treasure, especially anything gold, had irresistible appeal. And if engraved on the gold were mysterious hieroglyphics giving the history of the ancient inhabitants of this land, the story was all the more enticing. How could the strange writing be deciphered? Why, of course, Joseph Smith had a magic stone that he looked at in his hat and on which he could see anything—even the translation of ancient languages.

So it came to pass that the mysterious gold plates were "found." The "spirit" guarding them was an angel who led Joseph Smith to the priceless treasure; and after preventing him supernaturally during several abortive attempts, at the end of four years, the angel allowed him to take this ancient record because he had been chosen to restore true Christianity to earth. On a few occasions the plates were said to be under a blanket in the room nearby (no one could look upon them except Joseph) while the lengthy "translation" was in process. Joseph Smith didn't need to look at the plates, however; he looked into his hat, and there, shining on the "seer stone," were the hieroglyphics on one line and the translation just below. Usually the priceless plates were kept "hidden in the woods," for they were of little importance in the process. It was the "seer stone" that did it all, just as it had been doing marvelous things for Joseph for so long.

King James English in America in 600 B.C.

In the process of "translating" the Book of Mormon by means of his "peep stone" from hieroglyphics on "gold plates," Joseph Smith not only plagiarized several books about early

America that were popular in his day, but he copied entire chapters of the Bible. For example, compare Isaiah 2–14 with 2 Nephi 12–24; Isaiah 48 and 49 with 1 Nephi 20 and 21; and Isaiah 50 and 51 with 2 Nephi 7 and 8. Not content with that, Joseph Smith included, in portions of the Book of Mormon allegedly written in 600-500 B.C., hundreds of quotations from the New Testament. Perhaps he was too rushed, or else it didn't occur to him to paraphrase when plagiarizing. Consequently, the hundreds of quotations from both the Old and New Testaments (without acknowledging they were copied from Joseph Smith's Bible, but as though they came from the "gold plates") are all in King James English, 1500 to 2000 years before that edition of the Bible was published.

Remarkably, these passages of Scripture which the Book of Mormon Prophets allegedly received either independently from God or from ancient sources include not only the verse and chapter divisions from the King James Bible, but even the *italics* as well. How the Book of Mormon "Prophet" Nephi, who allegedly wrote 600 to 500 B.C. could not only quote Matthew, Luke, Peter, and Paul verbatim centuries before they wrote their gospels and epistles, but do it all in King James English as well, seems to allow only one explanation: The characters in the Book of Mormon were purely fictitious, and everything they said, including quotations from the Old and New Testaments, was written by Joseph Smith, who certainly had access to the King James Bible.

In Alma 46:15, believers are called Christians in 73 B.C., whereas Acts 11:26 says they were first called Christians at Antioch in about A.D. 42. The title "Christ" is used in the Book of Mormon, without explanation why Jews living in the Americas would use this Greek word instead of the Hebrew word "Messiah." In Ether 2:3, bees are said to be in America about 2000 B.C. yet they were first brought to the New World by the Spanish explorers. The absurdities, incongruities, anachronisms, and contradictions are too numerous to list here and have been covered by a number of authors.

The Myth-Defenders

Since the Book of Mormon is supposed to be an actual history of real people, places, and events on the North and South American continents, archaeology would seem the best hope for establishing Smith's credibility. Although events in the Bible go back much further in time than most of the Book of Mormon, the world's great museums contain huge quantities of evidence uncovered by archaeologists that verify Biblical history to the minutest detail. Yet not one pin or coin or piece of pottery has ever been found related to the Book of Mormon.

The Mormon Church is to be commended for financing, beginning in 1952, "the largest and most ambitious archaeological project ever funded by a religious institution (including the Vatican). . . ."[17] Known as the New World Archaeological Foundation, its first field directors were non-Mormons. As a result of the work sponsored by this Foundation, much valuable evidence has been uncovered that has increased knowledge about the early history of the Americas—but none of it comes even close to verifying anything related to the alleged peoples, places, or events recounted in the Book of Mormon.

Joseph E. Vincent gives some insight into the problems this has created: "At one time when I was a member of a ward bishopric, one of the counselors said to me: 'Why is it we have accurate maps of Palestine and not of the Book of Mormon lands? Why do we know so well where Jerusalem, Bethlehem and Nazareth are and do not know where Zarahemla, Bountiful and Cumorah are? Does that mean that actually those places are fictitious as the non-Mormons say they are?' "[18] Vincent tried to assure this man that "all is well in Zion," but it wasn't easy. Respected Mormon archaeologist Professor Dee F. Green has said:

> The first myth we need to eliminate is that Book of Mormon archaeology exists. . . . If one is to study Book of Mormon archaeology, then one must have a corpus of data with which to deal. We do not.
>
> . . . no Book of Mormon location is known with reference to modern topography. Biblical archaeology can be studied because we do know where Jerusalem and Jericho were and are, but we do not know where Zarahemla

> and Bountiful (nor any location for that matter) were and are.
>
> . . . a concentration on geography should be the first order of business, but we have already seen that twenty years of such an approach has left us empty-handed.[19]

The admission by Mormon archaeologists and anthropologists that no one knows the location of even one Book of Mormon city or geographical site, including the famous Hill Cumorah, is absolutely fatal to the claims of the Mormon Church and exposes the highest Church authorities, affectionately referred to by the masses as The Brethren, as brokers of fraud. The Hill Cumorah is allegedly the location where several hundred thousand warriors died in the last great Book of Mormon battle; where Moroni buried the fabled gold plates; and where Brigham Young claimed that there was, inside the hill, a huge cavern filled with wagonloads of gold plates. Yet the small hill near Palmyra, New York, which the Church identifies as Cumorah, has never yielded so much as one scrap of evidence of this great battle, nor has anyone ever been able to unearth even one gold plate (which would be one of the world's greatest archaeological finds and would prove the Book of Mormon).

Though divided on much, most Mormon archaeologists agree on one thing: The real Cumorah,if there ever was one, definitely was *not* located where Joseph Smith claimed he discovered the gold plates.

Beyond the Book of Mormon

Prophet Smith repeatedly declared that his miraculously given and translated Book of Mormon contained "the fullness of the everlasting gospel" that he had been called to restore. The Mormon Church is therefore in the uncomfortable position of having to take seriously the childishly naive and contradictory content of the Book of Mormon and the poorly conceived mythology concerning its "discovery." The embarrassing truth about an amateur fortune-teller named Joseph Smith, who was addicted all his life to seeking buried treasure and had been convicted of working a cheap scam, has to be suppressed.

What happens if questions are raised about the absurdities, grammatical errors, the contradictions, or the complete lack of archaeological evidence? These are taken care of by a subjective feeling that conveniently overrides common sense and all facts. The "burning in the bosom" is regarded as the manifestation of the Holy Ghost mentioned in Moroni 10:4. The Mormon missionaries' suggestion that prospective converts pray for this "burning" is extremely important in perpetuating the delusion of Mormonism because it sidesteps facts and substitutes feelings. The Book of Mormon promise is that those who "ask with a sincere heart" and have "faith in Christ" will receive this "sign." No one wants to be looked upon as insincere or lacking in faith, so there is a very strong desire to have this "feeling," which the very desire itself could psychologically create.

3

Temple Secrets

At the very center of the LDS faith are the Temples with their secret pagan ceremonies. Only in the Temple can the Mormon gain the secret knowledge and perform the occult rituals that allegedly bridge the chasm from human finiteness to eventual godhood. For most Mormons, the Temple is so sacred that anything said or done within its walls must be of God. What many Mormons themselves don't realize is that most of the Temple rituals are performed for disembodied spirits.

The ordinances practiced in Mormon Temples are of two types: those for the living, and the identical rituals done by proxy for the dead. The latter allegedly enable those who have been waiting in "spirit prison" for the millennium to become Temple Mormons. If the departed spirits choose to accept the proxy rituals, they are then allowed to go to the place called "Paradise," the home of all worthy Mormons who have died. The central importance of these ceremonies in Mormonism is emphasized in LDS scriptures. For example:

> And now, my dearly beloved brethren and sisters, let me assure you that

> these are principles in relation to the dead and the living that cannot be lightly passed over, as pertaining to our salvation.
>
> For their [the dead's] salvation is necessary and essential to our [the living's] salvation. . . .[1]

The Bible clearly teaches that death is final, and that those who die have no further chance to be saved: ". . . it is appointed unto men once to die, but after this the judgment."[2] For those who die without having received Christ as Lord and Savior, it is forever too late to be saved. Jesus said, ". . . if ye believe not that I am he, ye shall die in your sins . . . [and] *whither I go ye cannot come*."[3] Blatantly denying this, Mormonism teaches that, just as the Serpent told Eve, "You won't really die." In Mormonism, those who die aren't really dead but can still communicate with the living and join the Mormon Church beyond the grave.

Saviors of the World?

The Bible contains one verse that does refer to baptism for the dead. Pointing to this, Mormons say, "The Bible teaches baptism for the dead, and we baptize by proxy for the dead in our Temples. This proves that the Mormon Church follows the Bible and all other churches don't, so it must be the only true Church." Reading this verse in context, however, it becomes clear that baptism for the dead was not practiced by Christians, but by pagans.

In 1 Corinthians 15 Paul uses the pronouns "we" and "us" for 28 verses in speaking of and to Christians. Then in verse 29 he suddenly changes the pronoun to "they" when he says, "Else what shall *they* do who are baptized for the dead? If the dead rise not at all, why then are *they* baptized for the dead?"

It is quite evident that Paul is not referring to Christians but to the non-Christian pagans of his day, because he refers to them as "they," indicating some group other than the Christians to whom he has been speaking and addressing as "we" or "us." In verse 30 he changes the pronoun back again when he says, "And why stand *we* in jeopardy every hour?" Clearly the "they" in verse 29 refers to someone other than the "we" in verse 30. Since the latter, as is clear from the context, obviously includes himself and the Christians he is writing to, the former must refer to non-Christians—i.e., the pagan worshipers of Paul's day. Clearly Paul is using the fact that the mystery religions practiced baptism for the dead as evidence that even the pagans believed in life after death, which is what he now begins to argue for by other examples. Far from teaching baptism for the dead, the Bible points out that it is a pagan and not a Christian practice.

In our modern world, it is the Mormons' well-intentioned though pagan program for evangelizing the dead and performing secret rituals by proxy for them that is one of the major distinctives between Mormons and other religious groups. Indeed, the Mormons often point to this with pride. John Taylor, third President of the

Mormon Church, stated: "...we are the *only* people that know how to save our progenitors...we in fact are the *saviours of the world*, if they ever are saved...."[4]

Becoming Worthy

The secret Mormon path to "Godhood" winds back and forth through the Temple in repetition of occult ceremonies, 98 percent of which are for the dead. The most important of these is Celestial Marriage and "sealings" for eternity of family members to one another. According to Dr. Harold Goodman, President of the Mormon Mission in England:

> The goal of every Latter-Day Saint is to be married as a family unit in the "House of the Lord," and there receive these sacred blessings that will allow us eventually, if we're worthy, to dwell and be in the presence of our heavenly Father.
>
> We need to receive certain instructions, certain information and certain ordinances....That is the only way that we can be with Him to rule and reign with him. Otherwise, we could not be in his presence.[5]

How long will it take before Mormons can *eventually* gain access to the "presence of our heavenly Father"? Dr. Goodman doesn't explain, because not even Joseph Smith knew. That phrase "if we're worthy" represents a mammoth and undefined "if." Everything depends upon it, whereas the Christian's salvation depends upon Christ's worthiness, and the admission on his part that he is an unworthy sinner. According to the Bible, because Christ's sacrifice upon the cross has paid the full price for our sins that was demanded by infinite justice, every true Christian has instant access into the Father's presence through prayer; and upon death his soul and spirit go immediately to heaven.

Paul described this transition through death as "absent from the body and . . . present with the Lord."[6] When Christ returns, all those who have received Him as Savior and Lord will be "in a moment, in the twinkling of an eye . . . caught up together with them [the resurrected dead] in the clouds, to meet the Lord in the air; and so shall we ever be with the Lord."[7] Not so for the Mormon, who according to the "restored gospel," must struggle for "ages and aeons" to get *eventually* to heaven, if somehow he is able to become worthy enough to merit it.

To learn how to become "worthy" to do their Temple work, Latter-Day Saints attend special "Temple Preparation Seminars." Eagerly beginning these classes and expecting to learn at last what really goes on inside Mormondom's tightly guarded sanctuaries, the candidate is in for a perplexing disappointment. Instead of receiving specific instruction about Temple ceremonies, he finds that he is being prepared to face an unknown but crucial initiation ritual that he cannot be informed about in advance. Nor will he be informed, until he has been admitted inside the Temple, that he will be required to swear death oaths, for the forfeiture of his own life, should he reveal any of the Temple secrets.

Emphasizing loyalty to Joseph Smith and the Church he founded, 11 of the 12 Seminar lessons focus upon the personal worthiness required to become part of a secret circle of Mormon elite called "Temple Mormons." In the twelfth session the instructor finally discusses the actual Temple visit, but without revealing a single sacred secret. To the candidate's disappointment, his anxious questions continue to receive the by-now-monotonous response required in the instructor's manual: "You will learn the answer to *that* as you serve in the Temple." The closest the candidates come to learning that Temple work is really only the first step in a long and arduous journey is when they are given Brigham Young's instruction:

> Your endowment is to receive all those ordinances in the House of the Lord, which are necessary for you, after you have departed this life, to enable you to walk back to the presence of the Father, passing the angels who stand as sentinels, being enabled to give them the key words, the signs and tokens pertaining to the Holy Priesthood, and gain your eternal exaltation in spite of earth and hell.[8]

Tony and Debbie didn't get that far. While they were taking the Temple Preparation Seminars, so many serious questions were sidestepped by the instructor that this constant "You'll learn *that* in the Temple" began to sound evasive. Instead of answering questions, the Seminars were raising more questions and creating doubts. Why all the secrecy? And why wasn't there something in the Bible or at least in the Book of Mormon about Temple work? There were a few references in *Journal of Discourses* and *Doctrine and Covenants*, but nothing very revealing about the ceremonies. How could the Church expect Tony and Debbie to commit themselves to Temple work, yet refuse answers to honest questions? Tony told us:

> My wife and I knew that we couldn't obtain our exaltation to "Godhood" without going through the Temple, so we enrolled in a Temple Preparation class.
>
> Although the instructor wouldn't answer our questions about the Temple, we were learning that everything depended upon our becoming "worthy."
>
> One evening after coming home, we decided to see what the Bible said about the Temple and its ceremonies There was *nothing* in the Bible about "Christian" temples.
>
> However, in Romans 4 we read that

a man is justified by faith and not by works, and even that good works were a stumbling stone to those who try to pursue their salvation that way.

We really began to doubt that the Temple ceremony was Biblical, even though the Church had told us it was. Studying more, we found that the Bible was in serious conflict with Mormon theology and doctrine.

We went through a period where we were in a very depressed state. In order for us to accept what we were reading about the true and living Jesus Christ . . . we would be alienated from all of our friends and relatives.

We went ahead and decided that Jesus was to be the way, the truth, and life for our family.

The Staggering Burden of Perfection

Having completed the Seminar series, the candidate now vaguely realizes that inside the Temple he will be learning secrets and gaining mysterious Priesthood powers. If he learns and applies them *perfectly*, these will enable him to pass safely whatever fearsome tests await him in the spirit world and eventually to gain access to the heavenly Father's presence, perhaps in a few trillion years, when he has attained perfection. In spite of the joyful anticipation of entering the

Temple, a disquieting feeling that will grow into a heavy burden is settling upon him. He now realizes that regardless of whatever lip service Mormonism may give to Jesus Christ as Savior, the awesome responsibility for his own salvation, in the final analysis, rests upon him.

The most sobering realization is that nothing less than 100 percent *perfection* will do. The candidate now hopes fervently that the secrets he will learn in the Temple will give him the power to attain this perfection. President Spencer W. Kimball has written these words:

> This progress toward eternal life is a matter of achieving perfection.
>
> Living all the commandments [there are over 4300 in Mormonism] guarantees total forgiveness of sins and assures one of exaltation through that perfection which comes by complying with the formula the Lord gave us.[9]

In Mormonism, the blood of Christ atones for Adam's sin only, which brings resurrection to all, including animals and birds.[10] Christ's blood doesn't atone for a single individual sin,[11] which can be paid for only by 100 percent obedience to every command, or in some cases with one's own blood being shed, according to the "restored gospel."[12] Moreover, no one can be saved in ignorance.[13]

When they understand what is really involved in achieving "exaltation," many Mormons begin to have serious doubts about whether they want to become "Gods" and "Goddesses" after all. (In Mormonism, the woman can never become a god, only a goddess, eternally bearing children as one of many wives to a god-husband.) Unfortunately, for most Mormons it is too late to turn back at this point. They have committed themselves too deeply. The price would be too great in loss of friends, family, prestige, and self-esteem to back away from the Church. And what else is there, since all other churches are an "abomination"?

Point of No Return

Once inside the Temple, the candidate has just seconds to make decisions of eternal consequence. Like a blind person being led by the hand, he must now commit himself unreservedly to Joseph Smith and the Mormon hierarchy, or else abandon the Temple and all hope of "exaltation" in shame. This is when many Mormons want to cut and run, but few do. The candidate must commit himself to participate in still-unknown ceremonies, from which there will be no retreat, for he will be required to take death oaths vowing to forfeit his life if he reveals the Temple secrets. The programmed belief that the long-sought secrets of the Temple hold his only hope for gaining eternal life pushes him on despite unanswered questions and haunting doubts.

An inner conditioning process that has been going on for months or years is now reaching a climax beyond which there will be very little likelihood of ever consciously questioning The Brethren again, no matter how many red flags are waved by reason and conscience. There has been a blind commitment to Joseph Smith and the Church he founded ever since that "burning in the bosom," a willing surrender of one's mind to let the hierarchy do the thinking and dictate the demands. There have been moments of doubt, nagging questions that were put on the shelf. But once that step forward to participate in the Temple rituals has been taken, something clicks inside the soul, like a door being slammed shut, putting those questions forever out of reach. This is the final step, the full surrender to an endless path of self-righteous striving to be perfect that conscience has warned against again and again; but from now on conscience must remain silent like the lips that will be sealed with the death oaths of secrecy.

Having swallowed hard with determination to go through with it, the nervous initiate is in for several quick shocks. Husbands and wives, joyfully anticipating having their marriage "sealed" in the Temple for eternity, are immediately parted and will only come together briefly after having endured two hours of rituals separate from each other. Led first to men's and women's dressing rooms, they are instructed to strip stark naked. Oddly enough, each person *locks* his clothes in an individual locker, though no one but worthy Temple Mormons has access to the carefully guarded premises.

"Garment [underwear] of the Holy Priesthood"

After partially covering their nudity with a poncho-like piece of thin cotton completely open on both sides, to which the key to their locker is pinned, the "Temple patrons," as they are called, are led to the "washing and anointing" room. There Temple workers ceremoniously "wash" the various parts of their nude bodies with water, reaching under the open "shield," as it is called, and then "anoint" the initiates with oil in a similar manner. During this startling process, a singsong formula is recited by the Temple worker, bestowing a special blessing upon each body part being "washed" or "anointed." This is the preparation for being dressed in the "Garment of the Holy Priesthood," a sort of "magic underwear" much like an old-fashioned set of long johns with Masonic markings sewn into it.

To remain in good standing as a Temple Mormon who continues to perform the rituals essential in getting off to a good start on the infinite journey to "Godhood," both men and women must wear the magic underwear 24 hours each day for the rest of their mortal lives. Jim and Judy expressed their feelings after having worn these sacred long johns for years. "This garment is supposed to be all-magical and all-protective," said Jim, "keeping you from harm if you're living the gospel of the Latter-Day Saints."

His wife Judy added, "The garment is supposed to be worn next to your skin, and with other underclothes on top of that to protect your body. It's really just like wearing a rabbit's foot. It's a superstition."

Lucifer's Power and Priesthoods

In the dramatization of scenes from the Garden of Eden that Temple patrons watch, Lucifer instructs Adam and Eve that there is no way for them to gain the knowledge to become "as gods" except to disobey "Father" and eat of the forbidden fruit.[15] As we have already seen, Mormonism teaches that Satan told Eve the truth, that Adam and Eve didn't sin in disobeying God, and that the "fall" was really a "blessing in disguise" that opened the door to godhood for the human race. At this point in the Temple ceremony, which is derived largely from Masonic rituals, a fascinating sequence of events occurs.

Lucifer has appeared on the scene wearing an embroidered apron very similar to the one Masons wear. Partaking of the forbidden fruit and becoming "wise," Adam notices Lucifer's apron and asks him what it means.

Satan then replies, "It is the emblem of my power and priesthoods."

Having said that, Lucifer directs Adam and Eve to fashion similar aprons for themselves. He excitedly and slyly cries, "See, you are naked. Take some fig leaves and make your aprons. Father will see your nakedness. Quick! Hide!"

As obedient to Satan as they were disobedient to God, Adam and Eve follow the instructions of "the god of this world." As soon as Adam and Eve have tied their Luciferic aprons about them, the ceremony narrator instructs the Temple patrons to place their own fig-leaf aprons (part of the Temple costume brought with them or supplied) over their beautiful Temple clothing. As obedient to Satan as Adam and Eve have been, each Mormon going through the Temple solemnly puts on the fig-leaf apron. In contrast, the Bible indicates that God refused to accept Adam and Eve's fig-leaf aprons as a covering for their nakedness. Instead, He clothed them in the skins of animals that He had sacrificed for them as a symbol of the sacrifice Christ would one day make upon the cross for the sins not only of Adam and Eve but of the whole world.

Astonishing as it may seem, Temple Mormons are married and buried in this fig-leaf apron that their own doctrine identifies as the symbol of Lucifer's "power and priesthoods." This is only part of the fascinating legacy that Lucifer has succeeded in bequeathing to the Mormon Church.

As the dramatization continues, Temple patrons see Peter, James, and John sent by Elohim to rescue Adam and Eve, with no explanation how this could happen thousands of years before these apostles were born. These strange invaders from the future "prove" their identity by giving Adam and Eve the secret Masonic signs of the Mormon Priesthood. With Adam and Eve, the patrons advance to the Telestial Kingdom and the Terrestrial World, where they are put under covenant to obey more laws, and are taught their accompanying Priesthood tokens, names, signs, and penalties.[16] Here they are also clothed in the Robes of the Holy Priesthood and taught the "True Order of Prayer."

Now the patrons are given a "test" such as they will allegedly face in the hereafter. At an elaborate "Veil," they are challenged to give the secret signs and passwords which they have just learned, and only by doing so will they be allowed to pass through to the other side. The Jewish Temple at Jerusalem (after which Mormon Temples are supposedly fashioned) had a veil so heavy that it took many priests to raise it enough for the High Priest to enter once each year. When Christ cried upon the cross, "It is finished!" this veil was torn by the hand of God from the top to the bottom,showing that the way into the presence of God had been opened up through his sacrifice for our sins.[17] In Mormon Temples, however, this veil has been replaced by a flimsy, very thin, though beautiful, curtain. Divided into sections with a men's and women's side, the "Veil" has numerous holes and Masonic markings corresponding to those on the magic underwear.

Behind each segment of this elaborate curtain, a Veil Worker representing "the Lord" challenges each patron being led up and assisted through the ritual by a Temple Worker. Patrons are told that they will someday have to meet the Mormon "God" in this exact manner; and if they cannot then remember all the tokens, signs, names, penalties, they will not be allowed to enter into His presence. Reaching their hands through holes in the flimsy Veil, each patron assumes with "the Lord" on the other side of the veil the position of the "five points of fellowship" as in Masonry: inside of right foot to inside of right foot, knee to knee, breast to breast, hand to back and mouth to ear. In this "holy" position, the patron must perfectly repeat the following Mason's incantation: "Health in the navel, marrow in the bones, strength in the loins and in the sinews, power in the Priesthood be upon me and upon my posterity through all generations of time throughout all eternity."[18]

Since each patron is wearing the Luciferian fig-leaf apron which God rejected but Mormons have adopted, one need hardly wonder what power and what Priesthood the patrons are solemnly putting themselves under for eternity. In fact these oaths have put them in Lucifer's kingdom. Just before they received the Robes of the Holy Priesthood, the patrons listened solemnly as Lucifer gave forth with Mormon doctrine, warning them that, "If they do not walk up to *every* covenant they make at these altars in this temple this day, they will be in my power!"[19] No one except Jesus has ever perfectly kept the Ten Commandments. Certainly no Mormon can do that, much less maintain 100 percent obedience to every one of the thousands of laws in the "restored gospel." Therefore, every Mormon going through the Temple and making these covenants has placed himself by solemn blood oaths completely under Satan's power and in full submission to The Brethren.

What Good is a "Secret" That's No Longer Secret?

Mormons boast that their Temples are guarded by God and angels, and that no one who is not "worthy" can enter without detection and expulsion. This has been proven to be a vain delusion on more than one occasion, when a "Gentile" or an "Apostate" has gone through the entire Mormon Temple Ceremony with a hidden tape recorder undetected by the Mormon "Gods" and angels. The complete transcript with explanation has been published by former Veil Worker Chuck Sackett under the title, *What's Going On In There?*

This was done to show the folly of "secrets" that can't be kept secret. Now that the Mormon Temple secrets are no longer secret, will The Brethren change the Temple rituals to establish new secrets? By what authority and for what purpose? In exposing these former secrets, we only wish to help Mormons by demonstrating the folly of imagining that "secret" grips and signs are of any value. The God of the Bible looks into each heart, knows each thought, and neither needs nor honors the childish secret passwords that seem impressive to men. Jesus said:

> I am the good shepherd, and know my sheep, and am known of mine . . . and I lay down my life for the sheep . . .
>
> My sheep hear my voice, and I know them, and they follow me:
>
> And I give unto them eternal life; and they shall never perish, neither shall any man pluck them out of my hand.[20]

4

A Time to Choose

Out of genuine concern for those who are committed to or are seriously considering Mormonism, we have attempted to present the truth about what the Mormon Church really believes and practices.

Cindy discovered the truth for herself, but not until Mormonism had destroyed her marriage. With ancestors who had crossed the plains to Utah in handcarts, Cindy had been born into an LDS pioneer family and was an active Mormon for 30 years. Her husband, however, lost interest in the Church and wasn't living up to its standards. "He had no desire to be active in the Priesthood," Cindy told us, "so the Mormon leaders encouraged me to divorce him." It was in the midst of that trauma that Cindy began seeking some answers. Her story gives hope to others:

> As far as I was concerned, the Mormon Church was totally the right thing, and I would do whatever they said. I spent my entire life working in it and doing everything I could to promote it. I started teaching when I was 17 and was teaching seminary

> and genealogy when I finally left the Church.
>
> What happened was that I began to study the Bible and became aware that the god of Mormonism was not the real God of the Bible. He was a counterfeit, probably one of the best counterfeits that Satan has come up with to keep people away from knowing the real and living Jesus Christ.
>
> I had to make a choice, and I chose Jesus over Joseph, and being a Christian instead of becoming a goddess wife to some Mormon man/god.

Cindy's opinion that the Mormon "God" is a satanic counterfeit designed to keep Mormons from knowing the true God may seem harsh. However, there is more than enough documentation—not only from former Mormons but from Mormon Prophets and Apostles—to show that Mormonism is a Luciferian religion within the mainstream of anti-Christian pagan tradition. It is not even based upon the Book of Mormon, and is certainly not based upon the Bible. Brigham Young made the astonishing admission that he had "not read the Bible in years" and that when he had attempted to study it, he "did not understand the spirit and meaning of it. . . .[1] He further admitted that in his day the Twelve Apostles of the Mormon Church included men who believed in reincarnation, rejected the existence of God, and denied that there was any value in the death of Christ for salvation.[2] One would think that such admissions as these and the many others equally damaging that we have quoted would cause every Mormon to seriously reevaluate his religion.

Sadly, however, from The Brethren on down, Mormons generally have not responded well to constructive criticism. They are afraid even to consider momentarily the possibility that there might be any error at all in their church or its Prophets or doctrines. Any attempt to point out even the most obvious fallacies is met by the standard Mormon response: a wounded complaint that they are being attacked, along with the seemingly sincere protest that they attack no one. Mormons seem to forget that Joseph Smith declared all Christian creeds to be an abomination. Brigham Young said that all Christians were "grovelling in darkness,"[3] and that the Christian God is "the 'Mormon's' Devil. . . ."[4] John Taylor, third Mormon President, said that Christianity was "hatched in hell,"[5] and "a perfect pack of nonsense . . . the Devil could not invent a better engine to spread his work. . . ."[6] Continuously around the world, hundreds of times each day in secret ceremonies before thousands of Mormon Temple patrons, all Christian ministers are ridiculed and slandered as absolute fools who are hired by Satan to deceive their congregations.[7]

Clearly Mormonism from its very beginning has had a deep controversy with Christianity and has aggressively pressed its attack. The differences between the two are very real and need to be understood rather than denied. We have attempted to contribute to that understanding.

Notes

Chapter 1—Could Such Good People Be Wrong?

1. Milton R. Hunter, *The Gospel Through the Ages* (Salt Lake City: 1958), p. 110.
2. 1 Timothy 2:14.
3. Romans 5:12-21.
4. Romans 6:23.
5. *Deseret News*, Church Section, July 31, 1965, p. 7.
6. Ibid., June 18, 1873, p. 308.
7. *Doctrines of Salvation*, vol. 1, 1960 ed., pp. 113-15.
8. Bruce R. McConkie, *Mormon Doctrine* (Salt Lake City: 1966), pp. 516-17.
9. *History of the Church*, vol. 6, p. 306.
10. Joseph Fielding Smith, *Doctrines of Salvation*, vol. 2, 1960 ed., p. 86.
11. Ibid., pp. 87-89.
12. *Journal of Discourses*, vol. 16, p. 334; *The Seer*, p. 21.
13. *The Ensign*, "Jesus of Nazareth" by President Spencer W. Kimball, Dec. 1980, p. 3.
14. *The Seer*, edited by Orson Pratt, Jan. 1853–July 1854, pp. 37-38.
15. James E. Talmage, *Jesus the Christ*, pp. 6-8, 15-16; *The Seer*, pp. 50-54.

Chapter 2—Sifting Fact from Fancy

1. Walter Martin, *The Maze of Mormonism* (Vision House: 1978).
2. *The Prophet Joseph Smith's Testimony*, official booklet published by The Church of Jesus Christ of Latter-Day Saints, p. 3.
3. Ibid., p. 4.
4. *Dialogue: A Journal of Mormon Thought*, Autumn 1966, pp. 30-34.
5. Ibid.
6. *Doctrine and Covenants*, sec. 5, 1835 edition.
7. *Amboy Journal*, June 11, 1879, p. 1.
8. Jerald and Sandra Tanner, *The Changing World of Mormonism* (Moody Press: 1980), pp. 29-66.
9. *History of Joseph Smith*, by his mother, Lucy Mark Smith (Salt Lake City, 1945), pp. 91-92.
10. Ibid.
11. B.H. Roberts, *A Comprehensive History of the Church*, vol. 1, pp. 81-82.
12. *The Chenango Union*, Norwich, N.Y., May 3, 1877.
13. Dr. Hugh Nibley, *The Myth Makers*, p. 142.
14. Sworn Affidavit by Wesley P. Walters, Oct. 28, 1971: Leonard J. Arrington and Davis Britton, *The Mormon Experience*, pp. 10-11.
15. *Palmyra Herald*, July 24, 1822.
16. Reed C. Durham, Jr., typed syllabus published by the Church Educational System.
17. *Dialogue: A Journal of Mormon Thought*, "Mormons and Archaeology: An Outside View," Summer 1973, p. 45.
18. *Fourteenth Annual Symposium on the Archaeology of the Scriptures* (BYU, Apr. 13, 1963), p. 61.
19. *Dialogue*, op. cit., Summer 1969, pp. 77-78.
20. *Doctrine and Covenants* 20:9; 42:12; see also 135:3.

Chapter 3—Temple Secrets

1. *Doctrine and Covenants* 128:15.
2. Hebrews 9:27.
3. John 8:21-24.
4. *Journal of Discourses*, vol. 6, p. 163.
5. Personal interview for the movie *The God Makers*.
6. 2 Corinthians 5:8.
7. 1 Corinthians 15:52; 1 Thessalonians 4:17.
8. *Temple Preparation Seminar Discussions*, 1978 Edition (LDS Church publication), pp. 78,83.
9. Bernard P. Brockbank, *Commandments and Promises of God* (Deseret Book Co.: 1983); Kimball, op. cit., p. 208.
10. James E. Talmage, *Articles of Faith*, pp. 477-78; *Doctrines of Salvation*, vol. II, pp. 10-11.
11. *Journal of Discourses*, vol. 13, p. 143.
12. Ibid., vol. 1, pp. 97, 134-35; vol. 3, p. 247; vol. 4, pp. 49-54, 219-20; Bruce R. McConkie, *Mormon Doctrine*, p. 92.
13. *Doctrines of Salvation*, vol. 1, 1954, p. 303; *Doctrine and Covenants*, sec. 131, vv. 5-6.
14. Chuck Sackett, *What's Going On In There?*—The verbatim Text of the Mormon Temple Rituals annotated and explained by a Former Temple Worker (Sword of the Shepherd, P.O. Box 4707, West Lake Village, CA 91361), pp. 34-38.
15. Ibid., p. 27.
16. Ibid., pp. 34-46.
17. John 19:30; Matthew 27:51; Mark 15:37-38.
18. Sackett, op. cit., p. 52.
19. Schnoebeleu and Spencer, *Mormonism's Temple of Doom*, (Triple J. Publications, Idaho Falls, ID: 1987), p. 27.
20. John 10:11, 27-30.

Chapter 4—A Time to Choose

1. From an October 8, 1854, Conference discourse in which he clearly states that Adam is God. The Brethren have suppressed this and it is presently located in the LDS Archives in order to persist in denying that Brigham Young taught the "Adam-God Doctrine." Although the Mormon Church has never published this sermon, others have. This quote was taken from *Brigham Young 1854* (States West Publishing Co.: Scottsdale, AZ).
2. *Journal of Discourses*, vol. 12, p. 66.
3. Ibid., vol. 5, p. 73.
4. Ibid., p. 331.
5. Ibid., vol. 6, p. 176.
6. Ibid., p. 167.
7. Ed Decker, *The Temples of the God Makers*, 1985. A detailed analysis of the Temple ritual (Saints Alive, P.O. Box 1076, Issaquah, WA, 98027), pp. 6-8.

This booklet
has been excerpted from
Ed Decker's and Dave Hunt's unique exposé
on Mormonism:

The God Makers

This factual, carefully researched, and fully documented look at Mormonism provides staggering new insights that go beyond the explosive film of the same title. *The God Makers* is an excellent tool in reaching Mormons.

Available at
Christian bookstores everywhere.

ED DECKER, a convert to Mormonism at age 20, spent 19 years in the Church of Jesus Christ of Latter-Day Saints. He was a member of The Melchizedek Priesthood, a Temple Mormon, and active in many church positions.

DAVE HUNT has become internationally known for such significant bestselling books as *The Seduction of Christianity* and *America: the Sorcerer's New Apprentice*. A recognized cult expert, his research and consulting expertise takes him around the world.